THE COUNTRY ROAD

THE COUNTRY ROAD

POEMS BY JAMES LAUGHLIN

𝒵

ZOLAND BOOKS

Cambridge, Massachusetts

First Edition published in 1995 by
ZOLAND BOOKS, Inc.
384 Huron Avenue
Cambridge, MA 02138

SOME OF THESE POEMS FIRST APPEARED IN
Agenda (London), *Agni*, *Ambit* (London), *American Verse*, *Boulevard*,
Chelsea, *Conjunctions*, *Exquisite Corpse*, *Grand Street*, *Harvard Magazine*,
Harvard Review, *Hudson Review*, *Interim*, *Iowa Review*, *Loyalhanna
Review*, *The New Yorker*, *Parnassus*, *Poetry*, *Princeton Library Journal*,
Puckerbrush, *Sulfur*, *Threepenny Review*, *Vuelta* (Mexico City),
and *The Yale Review*.

Book design by Tree Swenson
Cover painting, "The Country Road,"
is by Marjorie Phillips

FIRST EDITION
This book has been printed on acid-free paper, and its binding
materials have been chosen for strength and durability.

Library of Congress Cataloging-in-Publication Data
Laughlin, James. 1914–
The country road : new poems / by James Laughlin. – 1st ed.
p.   cm.
ISBN   0-944072-46-1
I. Title
PS3523.A8245C68   1995
811'.54 – dc20   94-33669

for

LEILA & DANIEL

THE COUNTRY ROAD

THE DEPARTURE

They say I have to go away soon
On the long trip to nowhere.
Put things in order, they say.
But I've always been disorderly
So why start that now?
Not much time, they say.
What to do with it?
Not much different, I think,
Than what I've been doing.
My best friends have always been
The ones in books.
Read a few pages here, a few there.
No complaints, few regrets,
Thanks to everybody.

THE REVENANT

Others might call what I'm doing
Remembering but that's only the
Starting point. It's raining and
I'm lying on the living room sofa
Listening to some Mozart as I
Go over on the screen in my mind
Some of the things we did when
You were still alive. I see you
So clearly, it's almost as if you
Had just walked in and sat down
Near me. But then the real part
Begins. Yes, I repeat, the real
Part, our life together after
You had died. At first after
Your going I thought that every-
Thing was over. There were many
Empty months, long stretches of
Time when I didn't know what to
Do or where to go. And then, it
Was a miracle, something out of
Another world, you began to make
Your returns. The first time you
Came back (I marked it in my
Diary) was on the third of June
Two years ago. I couldn't touch
You of course though you looked
So real I put out my hand to
Try. You laughed and said, "Get
Up, you lazy man. It's a lovely
Day and we're going to take

A walk up to Old Man McMullen's
Pond; we can skinny-dip there
If there's no one around." And
So it was, the first of many
Times we've been out together.
Of course when people pass
Us they don't see you, they
Greet me as if I were alone.
That doesn't upset me since
I know you're there for real.
I never know ahead which days
You'll be coming but that's
All right, I know you'll come
Again when you can. I work at
Home in my old house at the
Edge of the forest. I'm more
Or less of a hermit and only
Go to the village for food
And the mail about twice a
Week. I think you're very
Generous with your time. I've
Stopped keeping track of the
Days we've had together. I
Don't venture to ask about
Your nights or where you go
When you leave me. We don't
Talk about things like that.
At first our jaunts were only
Here in the neighborhood.
Then you began suggesting
Places further away, some
Quite far away. Last March
It was the Arizona desert
When the wildflowers were
In bloom. I was frightened

About that trip; I had to
Go by plane; what if you
Couldn't get there or find
Me? But you didn't cause me
Worry, you were there at the
Tucson airport when I left
The plane. I had brought
Sleeping bags to camp out
On the floor of the desert
As I like to do every spring
If I can; the cooing of the
Desert doves is a sweet sound
Never to be forgotten. I had
Hopes you would stay with me
But you didn't. Half an hour
After the sun had set you
Promised you would be back
In the morning and dissolved
Into the darkness. One moment
You were there and the next
You weren't. I became more
Confident, I knew now I could
Rely on you. Our trips grew
Long and adventurous. In July
It was the little glacier inn
Above Zermatt and in August
The Due Torre in Verona. But
That was a mistake; we had
Stayed there once when you
Were alive and to be there
Without you was unbearable.

Are we getting too bold, are
We risking the happiness we
Have? For next year we're

Talking about India. When
You were alive we often
Dreamed of going to India.
I had been there but you
Never had. There would be
Days in Kashmir and the
Foothills of the Himalayas.
Jaipur and Benares, where
At dawn thousands bathe to
Wash away their sins. Puri
For the Jagannath festival.
The Caves of Ajanta with the
Buddhist saints smiling their
Eternal smiles. Konarak and
Khajuraho, where the stone
Lovers are forever embracing.
In the south the temples of
Chidambaram and Mahabalipuram.
Yes, we'll be going to India,
The land of all wonders and
Of fabulous transformations.
Sita, the wife of Rama, can
Become Ayonija or Lakshmi.
Siva is Nataraja and Rudra
And Mahadevi and many others.
Will we, in India, be also
Transformed? Will it even be
Granted to us that I may
Touch you and perhaps make
Love to you again?

REVENANT: *one who returns after death.*

IS MEMORY

Something we have
Or something we've lost?
How much remains of what
Happened when it first took place?
I imagine that I see you clearly,
Every detail of our first embrace,
That I still hear each word you spoke,
And the tones of your voice
As you spoke them. Yet how much
Of what comes back may be illusion,
Born of longing for what
Might later have been?

THERE'S NEVER
A NEVER

in love what once was
lovely can always return

when the storm clears or
the wind drives the clouds

away don't be hasty don't
lock the door of your heart

there's never a never in love.

WHO IS SHE?
WHO WAS SHE?

After forty years, perhaps more,
She has reappeared in my life
Of dreams, the beautiful woman
Dressed all in white, with long
Hair and a constant but enigmatic
Smile. The curious thing was her
Silence. She was mute. Though we
Were lovers, she never spoke a
Word to me. She was as quiet as
The night-shrouded grove of
Redwoods in which we used to
Meet. She was passionate but
Without a voice. Never a word,
But always smiling. I remember
Many things about her. She had
Soft and knowledgeable hands
When she caressed me. After an
Hour or so she would disappear.
One moment we would be enlaced
And the next she would be gone.
I would search for her among
The trees but she was not there.

Now that she has returned after
So many years, as real, as vivid
As ever, I hope that she'll enter
My world again, that she'll
Speak to me and tell me her
Name, tell me her story. I'd
Like to be able to summon her
When I have need of her love.

HERE IS MY HAND

take it in yours and open the
fingers to uncover the palm

study the lines of my hand
what do you see in them are

they veins of a leaf recording
some plan in nature that is be-

yond our understanding or are
they a map (roads crossing and

roads diverging) which tells
how our fates converged how

we were drawn to each other in
love how there were times when

we lost our way but then re-
joined to be always together.

ANIMA MEA

After we had made love
a girl with big eyes and
warm breath started to
talk about my soul hush
I said hush and beware
if I have a soul it's
only a box of vanities
tied with frightened
pieces of string.

ANIMA MEA: *my soul.*

LITTLE SCRAPS OF LOVE

Your letters, infrequent
But so sweet, so wandering
In what they relate, are
Little scraps of love.
What would I do without them?
They're food when I'm feeling
Hungry for you, so far away.
Please pick up your pencil
As often as you can, even if
It's only for a postcard.
And don't forget the childish
Pictures of us holding hands.

THE SEARCH

She writes that she cannot
Find me in her dreams. She
Has been searching for me
Night after night but with
No success. "Why are you
Hiding from me?" she asks,
"Did I do something to
Offend you, to hurt you?
I think you must have
Misunderstood what was
Meant as a sign of love."

"Look further, look deeper,"
I write her. "The world of
Dreams is vast. It has many
Passageways that lead to
Corners no one has ever
Visited. Don't abandon the
Search too easily. Don't
Give up. I have encountered
You in *my* dreams, beautiful
As you always were, your
Voice the same, unchanged.

"Yet what difference does
It make where we meet, in
Your dreams or in mine?
Does it matter if we are
Insubstantial? We still
Can speak the words we
Know, the words of love."

THE PRANKSTER

Who can foretell the pranks of that mischievous boy Eros?
    Who can guess at his whims?
Who knows where and when he will direct one of his joy-
    or pain-bearing arrows?

I have known sweet Nephrosyne for ten years,
The friend of my wife Portulaca,
The loyal wife of Ephrastus, my companion in arms,
The model of matronly virtues.
I thought of her as my sister, I confided in her and sought her
    counsel in matters of the heart,
I admired her beauty as I would that of a painting of Apelles.

And then, without warning, without any solicitation on my part
That dangerous boy launched one of his arrows;
True it flew to lodge in my heart, where it is embedded
And I cannot tear it loose even if I would.

Nephrosyne is no longer my placid sister, she is the object of my
    chalorous desires.
When she approaches I tremble with longing.
My eyes are riveted on her beauty, on the grace of her movements.
That boy's arrow has wounded me deeply.
Will it also bring me bliss?

EROS: *in mythology the boy god whose arrows kindled love.*
APELLES: *a Greek of the 4th century B.C., considered the greatest painter of*
    antiquity.
The other Greek names are fictitious.

THE COUNTRY ROAD

In the painting that hangs in our dining room
A country road, a dirt road, is winding up the slope of a
    mountain ridge;
It begins in pastureland and goes up through scattered trees to
    dense woodland.
It is a scene in western Pennsylvania near the farm where we
    went in summer
To get away from the heat of the city.

I say that the road "is winding," not "winds,"
Because, for me, the painting sometimes seems to be still in
    progress,
Though the dear lady who did it has been dead more than
    fifteen years.
Some days, if I'm alone as I pass through the room,
I may notice some very small alteration in the
    composition
As if the artist were still working on it.
A tree may have slightly changed its position in
    the landscape,
Or the farmhouse and barns in the middle distance;
A patch of color in the pasture or the cornfield of the foreground
    may appear different;
The contour of the mountain ridge against the sky has been
    moving.
Even in the direction that the road is taking, its curves are never
    precisely the same.
It's always a sun-filled scene, but the quality of the light may vary.

As my eyes walk that familiar road, where I walked so often
      as a child,
I see things I hadn't detected before,
Little things of no great importance, but I'm
      aware of them.

Oil painting of "The Country Road" was done by
    Marjorie Phillips in Western Pennsylvania about 1940.

A FLORILEGIUM

The Purple Clematis

Each day the purple clematis climbs further up the wire beside
    the kitchen door
Green fingers twine around the strands of wire
And soon there is another blossom with a yellow star at its
    center
Whom are you chasing, I ask the flower
Are you racing the horses of the sun?
Do you imagine that Phaëthon, son of Helios, has time to fall
    in love with you?
Surely you've heard that he is condemned to die every evening
How like a man, she answers, what do I care about the drivers
    of chariots?
I'm only looking for a small crack in this wall
Where I may conceal myself from that ruffian, the north wind
    Boreas
Who only too soon will be here with his cruel winter.

The Wild Geranium

How like a flower does Chloe gently bend her head
At the approach of wind or rain
Then comes the sun and quickly she's herself again
Not arrogant but confident of her beauty.

Anthea

Anthea greenly creeps the ground
Her tiny flower hardly to be seen against the rocks
But country people know of her healing power
Zeus promised it for her in recompense
When he forced her mother, the sweet nymph Cleomine.

FLORILEGIUM: *a collection of flowers.*
PHAËTHON: *in Greek mythology the son of Helios, the sun, who met his death trying to drive his father's chariot of horses across the sky.*
ANTHEA: *my name for my muse.*

the sheep in their feeding
have scattered from each

other and I see that they
have formed (white dots

against the green) the pat–
tern of the constellation

Canis Major which in the
night sky surrounds Sirius

the Dog Star Sirius the
dog of Orion the hunter

who was loved by Eos the
goddess of the dawn and

she had him stung to death
by scorpions because he

didn't requite her love.

BITTERSWEET

is the plant of jealousy,
Celastrus scandens, a woody vine
with small greenish flowers
succeeded by yellow capsules
which burst open when ripe
revealing its scarlet seeds.
Taste the seed and it is first
sweet but then turns very bitter.

Nature ordains that bittersweet
fasten itself upon other plants
and even trees; its hungry tendrils
twine voraciously around each twig
and branch to consume them.

Beware the bittersweet, dear girl.
Perhaps it may first give you
a sweet taste of vengeance,
but later it will embitter you,
rob you of joy, give you great pain.

Ἔροσ δηὖτέ μ' ὁ λυσιμέλης δόνει.
γλυκύπικρον ἀμάχανον ὄρπετον.

—SAPPHO

Eros once again limb-loosener whirls me
sweetbitter, impossible to fight off, creature stealing up
(I.P, fr. 130)

Sometimes when I can't fall asleep
I lie in bed trying to understand
What happened. I remember us so
Happy together, so many happy little
Things we shared that were quite
Apart from the glorious lovemaking.
And then...and then...The picture
Mists over, the details of the picture
Become unclear. There was never a
Quarrel, not even a disagreement.
There was certainly no intrusion
Of another person. I can't describe
What happened. It was as if clouds
Moved slowly across the sun but then
Didn't move on. It became a season
Of clouds as sometimes it is in the
Alps. No rain, no storm, just dark
Days, and nights when we were side
By side but some sort of screen
Was between us. I go over and over
It in my mind, trying to remember
Some conclusive incident. Did I,
Unconsciously, implant some fear in
You, fear of something that I
Couldn't recognize as part of me?
Something that made you feel pain
But I couldn't feel it? Did I come

Down with some hidden illness, some
Sort of genetic curse? Three years
Of loneliness. How can I hasten
The movement of the clouds across
The sun?

"When I was a boy with never a crack in my heart"

I roamed all roads, hungering to find out
What they meant when they spoke of love.
I was holding my heart in my hand,
Offering it to anyone who would take it.

She who was the first was older than I.
She knew men and their ways.
She had suffered from some who threw her away
  after their amusement.
Now she was seeking an innocent
Whom she could shape to her pleasing.

I will not condemn her;
She taught me so much that I had to learn one
  way or another.
But I soon began to fear her, beautiful and
  passionate as she was.
I knew she would alter me in ways I didn't
  want to accept.
It was only a matter of time till she would
  incise a crack in my heart,
A crack that would not quickly heal.
So I went on my way;
I took to the road again looking for another
  less demanding.

"When I was a boy . . .": from YEATS,
  "The Meditation of the Old Fisherman."

THEY ARE SUSPENDED

as if from the branch
of a giant oak their

bodies whirl in the
wind they are alive

but cannot reach out
to touch each other

they love each other
dearly but for some

reason it's impos-
sible for them to

come together they
can't embrace is it

a gallows from which
they are suspended?

WHY?

In an old letter found
in a drawer she mentions,
almost casually, marks on
her wrists, she writes that
"they can now hardly be seen."
Who? When? Why? that superb
girl, what agony was she
passing through?

THE RAIN ON THE ROOF

Tonight the small talk of the rain
Is speaking to us again.
It began as a storm,
Then quieted down into a steady patter.
It's a reassuring sound that tells us
Everything is going to be all right;
We'll wake up to good weather.

Each of us can hear in the rain-talk
Whatever voice we most want to hear;
Our mother's or that
Of a never to be forgotten lover.

When you turn over and wake
We listen together.
When you drift back to sleep
I lie watching you.
I listen to your breathing
And the rain-talk tells me
That our time together
Will always be happy.

"small talk of the rain": THOM GUNN.

CATULLUS XXXII

Ipsitilla, my sweet, dear girl,
Little furnace, send word at once,
Please, that I may spend the
Afternoon with you. And if I may,
Be sure no other cocks are let
Into your henhouse. And don't
You go walking the streets;
Stay home and have ready for me
Nine of your nicest continuous
Fucks. (And don't forget the
Wine.) May I come as soon as
Possible? I've had my lunch
But I'm hot for it and my
Prick is trying to poke holes
In my shirt and the blanket.

If the elegant Latin euphemisms are converted to
U.S. colloquial, this is what the poem says.

WHY DOES LOVE HAPPEN?

It's not so simple
As the biological imperative
To propagate, though
There's that of course.
But it's also the way you look
At me, your face alight with joy,
And the way your voice sounds
In the dark. What makes *my* love
Come to you? Once I asked
But you wouldn't answer. It was
Your secret. Keep it so.

THE LOST SONG

This song that I have made to tell of you,
"Made out of a mouthful of air,"
Who but I will ever sing it,
Who will know who made it,
Or for whom it was made?

"made out of a mouthful of air": YEATS,
"He Thinks of Those Who Have Spoken
Evil of His Beloved."

THREE KINDS OF PEOPLE

There are I–people
And we–people
And them–people.
My son Robert, the one who killed himself
When he was twenty-two,
Was an I–person
From the time he was fired from first grade
For upsetting the other children,
And at the next school
The boys locked him in a sports locker
Because he was so objectionable
And he was there for six hours.
I'm an I–person too,
But less obnoxious than poor Robert,
Saved because I've had loving we–people around me,
Three wives and a peerless daughter.
My son Henry is a them–person to the core.
He doesn't have to work at it,
It's natural to him, as if it were in his blood,
To see what other people need for their well-being
And put that ahead of his own comfort and desires.

THE WOMAN IN THE PAINTING

(For Vanessa)

Cries to the artist who has just finished
Her portrait: talk about me, write about me,
Give a lecture. I want everyone to know
How important I am, how important it is
That you've painted me the way you have.
They must recognize the forms in my body,
The interplay of colors and shapes.
If you must you can even bring in
Mondrian's theosophy and Sacred Geometry.
I'm not content to be silent on
The museum wall, let me speak
As well as be beautiful.

Are at each other again.
Belinda had been sending out her dinner invitations,
Inscribed in calligraphy by her secretary
And delivered by the chauffeur in the Rolls, accompanied by
      a rose.
Pulcheria is now sending hers garlanded by a rare orchid.
Belinda has adopted a fashionable hospital
For which a splendid charity ball will be held at The Waldorf.
Pulcheria is more intellectual;
She has taken a literary academy under her bountiful wing
At which she will reign over a conference of international
      scholars
Who will dispute the ever vexing problem of whether poetry
Should be made of truth or beauty.

And what do the husbands think of this competition of the
      graces?
They have gone back to their offices to make more and more
      and more money.
They are delighted that their pretty little women have
Found ways to amuse themselves so harmlessly.
They chuckle to each other about it.

"Conspicuous waste," as Thornstein Veblen described it.
THORNSTEIN VEBLEN: American economist and social critic
    (1857–1929). He pioneered in studying the role of technicians
    in modern society.

A DIFFICULT LIFE

My mother referred to it
as "the unpleasant side

of marriage" when she was
thirteen a crazy man jump-

ed out of the bushes along
Woodland Road and exposed

himself a profound love
of Jesus carried her through

a long life which was dif-
ficult to bear I tried to

love her as much as I could
but I'm afraid I didn't add

much consolation to it I
threw the novel of her fa-

vorite author Lloyd C. Doug-
las out the window of the

train telling her it was
junk she was past tears.

IN THE SECRET GARDEN

Melchior Dinsdale was Euphemia's favorite poet, bar none.
From the day when Miss Applegate had first pointed out his
work in the Pegasus Junior High Anthology Euphemia had
thrilled, throughout her being, to the poet's intimations
of sensuality and expression of unbridled passion. She
trembled as she read his sonnets. Many of them she memorized.
Sleepless, she would lie abed reciting the chants of sacred
(and profane) love, imagining that they might have been
written to her. If only she could share her admiration, and
her longing, with the venerable poet himself. Surely he
would not be totally unresponsive to her deep feeling.

How great then was Euphemia's excitement when she received
word from her aunt, Lady Parfait of Bladderstone Hall, that
the Laureate would soon be visiting at the Hall, and that
Euphemia might be one of the party if she so desired.

How will this story end? Will Euphemia find happiness?
Or will she be defiled, her heart broken, as has happened
to others before, by the licentious old poet?

MR. HERE & NOW

I love words, I eat words,
But I don't chase them
Like the poet Carruth,
Who when he was young
Studied a page of the
Big Webster every morning.
I like to find a new word
By serendipity, a word
That has been waiting for me
In some book, and if it
Pleases me when I've looked
It up, it becomes part
Of me like one of the pimples
On my skin which I like to
Scratch for the fun of it
The way some children do.

Today's new word was
Haecceity (2 "c"s in the
Middle), hardly a melopoeic
Word. It's quite hard to
Pronounce. But it has much
Substance because it means
Thisness (and by later usage
Here and now.) It comes from
The Latin pronoun *haec*,
Which means *this*. Just remember
Hic, haec, hoc from school.
What's more substantial than

A *this*; it's closer to us
Than a *that*. If you have a
This you have something you
Can grab hold of, that won't
Slip away from you, that may
Persist as long as you're
Around in the here and now.

I found the word in a book
By a very learned Irishman
Of letters who is reputed to be
A bibulator of prowess. To show
His education he had put the
Word in Latin as *haecceitas*.
I knew at once that this strange
Word would be part of my permanent
Verbal paraphernalia, not to
Toss it about indiscriminately,
Not to use it to show off,
But to hold it in store for
The pleasure of a word–pal
With whom I correspond, who
Will know that I'm praising
His rare *thisness* and thanking
Him for being my Mr. Here & Now.

Has lain on a side table
In the living room for years,
Now seldom read, though Mary
Dusts it once a week. It's
Aubrey's *Brief Lives*. John Aubrey
Of Wiltshire and Trinity College
(1626–97). He knew everybody who
Mattered and etched them tersely
In immortal thumbnails; got down
"The significant scraps" about
Them. It was Auden who told me
About Aubrey, that summer we were
Teaching at Beloit. "He'll tell
You more about a person in a
Sentence than most writers
In a page." Dear, crinkly-faced
Auden. Evenings he would sit
At the college's out-of-tune
Piano banging out *Carmen*,
Singing the words in a hideous,
Raucous voice. Aubrey and Auden,
Two great, good men gone down.
And what will I leave? Typing.
A lot of foolish typed pages.

HOW DID LAURA TREAT PETRARCH?

The contemporary records are somewhat vague.
They speak of her beauty and her devotion.
The poems to her have romantic imagery,
But they don't get down to the nitty-gritty.
Did she mend his socks? Did she put up
With his tantrums? Did she make copies
Of his poems? Rub balm on his sore neck?
These are important questions for today's poets
As they set about to choose a life's companion.

PETRARCH: *Francesco Petrarca (1304–1374), the great Italian
poet and humanist of the Renaissance. His sonnets immortalized
the anonymous "Madonna Laura," his lifelong inspiration, who
may have been the wife of a Provençal nobleman.*

"La belle giovanetta, chóra e donna . . . *The beautiful girl that
was my lady . . ."*

Les trésors de la vieillesse
Sont les petites aventures
de l'imagination.
Un beau visage fait revenir
un autre
Qu'on a bien aimé loin dans
le passé.
Alors on se console en disant
"De nouveau je suis jeune."

The treasures of old age
Are the little adventures
of the imagination.
A beautiful face recalls
another
That was so much loved
long ago.
And we console ourselves
Saying, "I'm young again."

THE MERCY IN IT

An old man gone weak in the legs,
Who once danced the hours away,
Must now be content with his books
And what the poets say.

Let him sit in his chair in the sun
And watch how his flowers are growing,
There muse on the past
And on truths that are still worth knowing.

Let him walk with his cane by the lake,
Where the water so slowly moves,
Hearing talk in the clouds
That tells of his heart's old loves.

Parody of Yeats.

PERMANET MEMORIA

Age has done its dreaded work.
We are no longer what we were
When we met by the Aegean shore
And discovered we loved one another.
Now our hair is white and our limbs
Are weak, our skin is wrinkled,
There is no desire to be satisfied.
But there is still memory.
Let us give thanks to the kind god
Who provides the consolation of memory.
We can enflesh ourselves in memory.

PERMANET MEMORIA: *the survival of memory.*

GRANDFATHER

Sits on a chair at the
Kitchen table shelling
Peas into a bowl. He
Looks contented, even
Happy, smiling as he
Works. If you ask him
A question he probably
Won't answer. He has
No idea what my name is,
Or even, I guess, that
I'm his grandson. He's
93 but he has to be kept
Busy or he'll start to
Root around in closets
All over the house. What
Does he think is lost?
No matter, he has been
Asked to shell peas.
He's happy doing it. And
We'll have peas for lunch.

IT'S DIFFICULT

For him to walk very far now
Even with his cane. His steps
Waver as if they can't decide
Which way to go. What he likes
Best is to lie in the sun on
The long chair meditating. If
The sun is bright he tips his
Hat over his eyes. He lets his
Mind wander. He doesn't want
To think about what is going
On in the world, the killing,
The endless killing. He knows
It has always been so from
Time immemorial and nothing
Can be done about it. Century
After century it will go on;
It's the nature of the beast.
He lies in the sun with his
Eyes closed rereading in his
Mind all the books he has
Most loved. Scene by scene
and character by character
He relives them. This morning
It was that idiotic French girl
Who desperately wanted what she
Could never hope to have and
Ended up eating arsenic. This
Afternoon it may be fables in
Ovid: Persephone raped off

To the underworld and her
Mother wandering over half
The earth in search of her;
Theseus and abandoned Ariadne;
Orpheus and limping Eurydice,
Two ladies who didn't have
The best of it. Or that love-
Silly Russian woman who gave
Up her son for a rotten man
And threw herself on the tracks
In front of a locomotive. It's
His consolation that there
Are more books he loves to
Think about than there are
Days he's likely to need them.
Good or bad, foolish or brave,
As they may be, the book people
Are his true friends. They are
There in his mind to help him
Get through his difficult days.

IDIOTIC FRENCH GIRL: *Flaubert's Emma Bovary.*
The Greek girls are all in Ovid's Metamorphoses.
LOVE-SILLY RUSSIAN WOMAN: *Tolstoy's Anna Karenina.*

A TOAST TO THE
FORGOTTEN POETS

Everyone reads Simonides
and Alcaeus but who re-

members Diarchus of Cor-
inth Horace and Catullus

will be singing as long as
time lasts but what of the

sweet-tongued Stereus who
drowned himself in the Tiber

the poets of the Pléiade
have statues in every pro-

vincial town square Henri
Ladoule hasn't even an alley

named for him in his native
village in Picardy Shake-

speare has been translated
into every language but the

Bantus know nothing of George
Jarvis author of *Dialogues*

with Satan O brothers in
obscurity I drink to you

my companions yes I shall
join you soon in oblivion.

Simonides and Alcaeus were famous Greek poets;
  Horace and Catullus were Roman.
THE PLÉIADE: *a group of neoclassical French poets*
  in the 16th century; Ronsard and du Bellay were
  the most famous.
Diarchus, Stereus, Ladoule, and Jarvis are all fictitious.

SOME AMATORY EPIGRAMS
FROM THE GREEK ANTHOLOGY

Melissa pulled one reddish hair
From her braid and tied my hands
With it. I was her prisoner. I
Told her never to let me go.

Paulus Silentiarius (V, 230)

Sometimes secret love affairs
Yield more honey than those
Which are open.

Paulus Silentiarius (V, 219)

She kissed me one evening with
Wet lips; her mouth smelt sweet
As nectar. I'm drunk with her
Kiss. I have drunk love in
Abundance.

Anonymous (V, 305)

Melissa's beauty is the gift of
The god Eros; Aphrodite charmed
Her bed; the Graces gave her grace.

Meleager (V, 196)

In my heart Eros himself created
Sweet-voiced Melissa, the soul
Of my soul.

Meleager (V, 154)

Might it not be that someday in
Legend soft-gliding Melissa will
Surpass the Graces themselves?

Meleager (V, 148)

I swear, I swear it by Eros, I
Would rather hear her whisper in
My ear than listen to Apollo
Playing his lyre.

Meleager (V, 141)

I held her close, we were breast
To breast, hers supporting mine,
Her lips joined with mine. As for
The rest, the little bedlamp was the
Only witness; I am silent.

Marcus Argentarius (V, 128)

Her kiss is like the lime that
Catches birds. Her eyes are fire
And when she looks at me I also burn.
If she touches me she has me caught fast.

Meleager (V, 96)

I wish I were a rose, a pink rose,
For you to pick and press against
your snowy breasts.

Anonymous (V, 84)

Beauty without charm is only pleasing.
It's nothing to remember. It's like
Fishing with bait but no hook.

Capito (V, 67)

We fell in love, we kissed, you gave
Yourself to me, we had much pleasure.
But who am I, and who are you? How
did it happen that we came together?
Only the Kyprian goddess knows.

Anonymous (V, 51)

Gray are her lovely eyes, her cheeks
Of crystal. Could you not call her
Sweet mouth a rose? Her neck is of
Marble, her breasts smooth as marble.
Her small feet? They are more charming
Than those of silver-footed Thetis.

Rufinus (V, 48)

For so long, my darling, I prayed to
Have you with me at night, touching
And caressing. And now your love has
Brought me that happiness. You are
Beside me, naked. But why do I become
Drowsy? I owe you this felicity forever.

Rufinus (V, 47)

Beware a girl who is too ready.
But also one who hangs back too
Long. One is too quick, the other
Too slow. Look for one who is
Neither too plump nor too thin.
Too little flesh is as bad as too
Much. Never run to excesses.

Rufinus (V, 42 & 37)

Whether you have colored your hair
Dark or have it its natural shade,
It frames your dear face in beauty.
The god Eros loves your hair and
Will still be twining his fingers
In it when it is gray.

Anonymous (V, 26)

Shall we take a shower together,
Soaping ourselves and rubbing each
Other, flesh to flesh; then put on
Our robes and sip a good wine? The
season of such joys is short; then
Comes old age and finally death.

Rufinus (V, 12)

Make the bedlamp tipsy with oil;
It's the silent confidant of things
We seldom dare to speak of. Then
Let it go out. There are times when
The god Eros wants no living witness.
Close the door tight. Then let the
Bed, the lovers' friend, teach us
The rest of Aphrodite's secrets.

Philodemus (V, 4)

THE KYPRIAN: *Aphrodite was born on Cyprus.*
THETIS: *in Greek mythology one of the Nereids (sea nymphs), the mother of Achilles.*

APOKATASTASIS

The notion that after death all things recur in eternal
simultaneity — Unamuno makes a great case for it.

I wandered up there above the clouds,
Or was it down on the far shore of Lethe?
I wasn't lonely because everyone
Who'd ever lived whom I wanted to know
Was there, still alive but aethereal:
Sappho and Propertius, Rochester, even
Bertran de Born, all there and talking
Happily together, no fights now, poets
Of many tongues, complete simultaneity,
Like the new tricks they're going to do
With television. A cacophony, you ask,
Deafening, so much wisdom sounding
Together? No, it wasn't that at all.
It was like happy bees humming
In the meadows near Olympia, or like
The music of the spheres, but a music
Without trumpets or tympani, a gentle
Susurration that rose through the moon's
Light and past the orbit of the sun
To a distant galaxy where creatures
Not like us were listening for it.

UNAMUNO: *Miguel de Unamuno (1864–1936), Spanish*
   existentialist philosopher.
SAPPHO ET AL: *poets of different times and cultures.*
OLYMPIA: *a plain in Greece that was an important religious*
   center during antiquity.

Eros has broken his bow,
He has had to send it to the shop
For repairs, but he's still
Starting conflagrations of the heart
By rubbing dry sticks together.
Who here in the village
Would have dreamed it possible
That those two could have become
What the gossip columnist of the
Goshen Star calls an "item"?
Lump-faced Louella who's retired
From teaching social sciences
In the gradeschool; she received
A medal from the State Department
Of Education for forty years
Of devoted service. And bibulous Bob
Who never kept a job for more
Than a year but everybody loves him.
Now he lives on welfare. Eros smiles
Io Hymen . . . Hymenaeus Io!
It's a happy sight to see the two
Antique lovers strolling hand in hand
Along the village street, not to
The bar, love has put Bob on the
Wagon, but to the pizza parlor.
Io Hymen . . . Hymenaeus Io!
Their wedding has been announced.
Our beloved First Selectman will

Preside at the ceremony in the
Town Hall. Everyone in the village
Will come to wish them well.
Io Hymen . . . Hymenaeus Io!
Will Eros be hiding in the back
Of the room scanning the faces
For his next triumph?

Catullus LXI

HYMEN: *in Greek mythology Hymen, son of Apollo
and Urania, is the god of marriage. "Hymenaeus Io" is
the refrain in Catullus's epithalamium for the wedding of
his friend Mallium.*

HER HAIR

For several years I've been casting
Covert amorous glances at Berenike.
Ones her husband won't notice but
I hope she does. Though she never
Gives any sign of recognizing my
Ardor. Berenike has the most
Enticing hair I've ever seen on
Any woman. She is much in my
Fantasies and performs superbly
In them. But I fear that if once
She welcomed me to her bed that
Might be the end of my obsession.
What if she puts her flowing
Tresses in curlers at night? It
Would do for two or three times, of
Course, so as not to hurt her
Feelings, but then it would be
Over. Better things as they are.

BERENIKE: *in a poem by Callimachus she is the wife of
Ptolemy III, the king of Egypt. It's a long story, but her
comely tresses end up as a constellation in the night sky. See
Catullus LXVI, the* Coma Berenicea (The Lock of
Berenike), *Pope's* Rape of the Lock, *and Racine's play*
Bérénice, *in which she has become the lover of the Roman
Emperor Titus.*

PENELOPE VENIT
ABIT HELENE

It was raining during her lunch
hour and to keep dry she went
into one of those shabby little
theatres near Times Square.
In the next seat was a well-
dressed benevolent looking
gentleman perhaps in his sixties.
Because he resembled her father
back in Des Moines she did not
feel frightened when he took
her hand and drew it to his
waist. Such a nice old man.

           (after Martial, Ep 1.62)

*Update of a famous poem by Martial. A noble
Roman lady goes to the baths at Baiae, which were
notorious for loose morals. She enters the place as
virtuous as Penelope, the wife of Ulysses, but leaves
it a slut like Helen of Troy.*

THE WOOD NYMPH

(for Erica)

Sometimes when I am working
In the forest clearing brush from
The hemlocks, a wood nymph approaches
Walking her two small dogs.
Soft-footed and undulant she glides
Through the trees, a figure of grace,
A nymph of surpassing beauty.
Sometimes in her passage she'll stop
To greet me. *Xaire,* she says, *xaire
Broté;* greetings to you, mortal man.
Clear-voiced, she speaks as if
She were singing. She tells of
The spirits that inhabit the marshes.
She is the guardian of those who
Live in bogs and wetlands.
She never identifies herself
But I think she may be Melissa
of Kalymnos, the child of Athena
By a mortal named Euclidon; she
Was renowned for her singing.

MELISSA AND EUCLIDON: *fictitious characters.*

DOES LOVE LOVE ITSELF

The most? Sometimes I've suspected
That may be true. A new person comes
Into my life (and I into hers). We
Are together as much as possible,
Discovering who we are and what we
Can be to each other. No day but has
Its little adventure of the feelings.
But then as we become more habitual,
The thought may occur: what is it
That is really taking place? Am I
In love only with her, or am I,
Like the insatiable Don in Mozart's
Opera, infatuated with the idea of
Being in love again, of being
Attached to someone new? Is the god
Eros self-regardant? That busybody
Of the myths, did he, like Narcissus,
Become his own mirror? Does love
Love itself the most?

Narcissus: *in Greek mythology a beautiful youth who fell
in love with his own image in a forest pool. He died of his
vanity. The story is in Ovid's* Metamorphoses.

L'ENGLOUTI

How deep is the pit? Is it bottomless?
I thought I had touched bottom. I felt
I had drowned when Hermione, a girl
Whose wit was her wealth, let herself
Be seduced by the gold of the vulgar
Herondas. But worse was to follow.
Next it was Euterpe, wildly passionate
Euterpe, who destroyed me with her discovery
That she prefers girls to men. My friends
Commiserate but I'm past consolation:
Englouti is the French word for my
Condition. I'm afraid to return to the city.
What further disaster may await me there?

L'ENGLOUTI: *the drowned man.*
The Greek characters are fictitious.

HER HEART

(for Anne Carson)

is a volcano in eruption
many fearless men have perished there
Menippus of Macedonia, Sardonicus of Tyre,
Cyaxeres the Mede, Kartikeya, lord of the Hindu Kush,
their valor aroused admiration
but their fates were sealed
from the moment they laid eyes on her.
It was like the game called "the vizier's choice"
at the court of Aurangzeb.
They were dazzled by her beauty
and lost all power of judgment.
After their pleasure, they slipped
into her fiery crater
and were consumed.

MENIPPUS ET AL.: *fictitious characters.*
AURANGZEB: *17th-century Mogul emperor of India. A tough nut;
he gained the throne by defeating his three brothers and impris-
oning his father, Shah Jahan.*

SHE DOES NOT WRITE

Though she must know her silence
Is a painful burden for me to bear
(*Un fardeau grave*, as the French would say).
When we said goodbye at the station
There were little tears on her cheeks
(*Des larmes de tendresse*).
But that was ten days ago
And she has not written
(*Aucun petit mot pour me dire
Quelle pensait à moi*).
Is she already forgetting
What passed between us?

UN FARDEAU GRAVE: *a heavy burden.*
DES LARMES DE TENDRESSE: *tears of tenderness.*
AUCUN PETIT MOT . . . : *not even a word to tell me she's
thinking of me.*

A ROOM IN DARKNESS

Night is a room darkened for lovers.
The sun is gone, and our daytime concerns
and distractions with it.
Now in the darkness we are close together
As lovers are meant to be.
Whether we sleep or wake
Nothing intrudes between us.
We are soothed and protected
By the darkness of our room.

The first line comes from William Carlos Williams,
 "Complaint."

BELIEVE ME

There can be shadows in the dark
Not many can see them
But a lover can see them
As he waits for the beloved to join him
And a lover can hear even the fall
    of a naked foot
As the beloved approaches
He can hear the soft breathing
That is rising in expectation
As he stretches out his hand in the darkness
To welcome her to the place of love.

A SECRET LANGUAGE

I wish I could talk to your body
Less cautiously; I mean in a
Language as forthright as its
Beauty deserves. Of course,
When we make love there is the
Communication of touch, fingers
On Flesh, lips on innermost
Flesh, but surely there must be
A kind of speech, body in body,
That is even deeper than such
Surface touching, a language
I haven't yet learned, or haven't
Learned well enough, hard as
I've tried. Will I ever master
That secret language for you?

THE IMMANENCE
OF YOUR BODY

It's nearly three years since we've been together,
Since we made love.
The circumstances of life have kept us apart.
But tonight as I sit here in half-darkness,
Listening to the *Four Last Songs*,
Remembering things about you,
I'm convinced of the immanence, the indwelling,
Of your body in mine.
You're a part of me again.
I feel your every touch.
I can feel the warm pressure of the flow
Of your bloodstream against mine.
I pray that my body is equally
Immanent in yours,
That we have not heard our last song.

FOUR LAST SONGS: *by Richard Strauss, Schwarzkopf
singing them.*

LA VITA NUOVA

Thanks to my Virtual-Reality headset
I can now embrace her back at the same
time as her front.
Love expands; it was never like this
in the days of Catullus.

EROS RIDENS

When they make love it's hard
For her to keep serious about
What they're doing. She can be
Passionate for a few minutes
As they pleasure each other
But then she'll begin to laugh.
It strikes her how comical are
The movements of bodies. "You
Are like a lizard." She'll say,
"A squirmy lizard." And she'll
Laugh that delicious laugh. Yet
The more she mocks their play,
The more he loves her; the more
She makes them both so happy.

EROS RIDENS: *the love god is laughing.*

THE WRONG MAGIC

When you went away
My youth went with you
Everything happy from childhood on
Had come together in you

Why couldn't I hold you?
I tried so hard to work a magic on you
But I wasn't sorcerer enough
It wasn't, I guess, the kind of
magic that spoke to you
Or perhaps it wasn't magic at all
Just my illusion of magic.

THE CHANGE

when it came was nothing sudden
it was so gradual they didn't

notice it was coming and when
it began they weren't aware it

was happening it wasn't some-
thing they talked about at all

it began with such little things
like the way she kissed and how

long a kiss would last and what
her tongue would no longer do

(until there were no more kisses)
then where she wanted him to touch

her and what she wanted to touch
such gradual little differences

such an undeliberate alternance
in her tactile affection it was

as if nothing was changing with
intention sometimes there would

be a little change of tone when
they were talking she lost in-

terest in some of her prettiest
dresses replacing them with ones

that were less colorful and more
severe it was all so tentative

as if she were groping then one
day they realized (both at the

same time) it was something they
could speak of could bring into

the light but there was no bit-
terness no recriminations they

knew they would always be to-
gether the best of it would

always be the same that was
assured but each would be free

to act without asking as the
change would require of them.

DO THEY MAKE LOVE?

Don't pick at it, my nurse says,
It won't get well if you pick at it.

I've never seen him but I think
I know what he looks like.

I know it itches but if you don't
Leave it alone it will get worse.

I can't guess what he says to her
But I hear what his voice sounds like.

Remember what happened to Albert,
His leg got infected from scratching.

I don't dare imagine that he touches
Her, or that she touches him.

Albert had to go to the hospital,
They nearly had to amputate his leg.

If he touches her I want him to die.

BY THE IRISH SEA

These tired old waters
that today so softly

caress the shingle are
full of history for me

Saint Patrick bringing
the cross to the pagan

Gaels the wretched Span-
iards of the Armada drown-

ing as their ships broke
up in the great storm

and my own people sailing
from Scotland to Ireland

to find a new home in the
Pale in the troubled time

of Bonnie Prince Charlie
but the message the sea

gives me now is a happy
one that soon I'll be

flying over these waters
back to you my true and

bonnie lass back to you.

BONNIE PRINCE CHARLIE: *Charles Stuart, Scots*
    "Pretender" to the throne of England (1720-1788).
THE PALE: *in the 14th century the English, who*
    controlled the land around Dublin, built a great
    wooden fence, many miles long, to protect
    themselves from the wild Irish, whence the saying
    "beyond the Pale."

THE RISING MIST AT ARD NA SIDHE

When I awake at dawn, at the *alba*,
A soft mist is rising from Loch Caragh.
Ta ceo bog ag eiri on loch.
It fingers up from the garden through the trees.
It is reaching for Macgillicuddy's Reeks,
The mountains that stand up from the lake.

The scene could be a Japanese scroll painting
Of Lake Biwa and the hills beyond Kyoto.
But this is not Japan, it is Ireland.
I've not been sleeping on a tatami
With the little wooden pillow block under my neck.
Ketsin is not beside me in the room with walls
                    made of paper.

They wrote me with great respect that Ketsin had died;
That was some forty years ago, she had died in childbirth.
(But this is not Japan, it is Killorglin.)
The slight form of Ketsin is not near for me to touch.
Her frightened smile and her almost inaudible voice
                    no longer compose a person.
She will not have twined flowers into my western shoelaces.
She will not bring me my wake-up tea.
She will not ask the morning question:
"Are you awake now, my lord?"

ALBA: *Provençal, the dawn.*
TA CEO BOG . . .: *repeats the title in Irish.*

73

LOST

Some of my friends have all
The luck when it comes to
Dreams. They have such a variety
Of wonderful, exciting dreams:
Dreams about sexy mysterious
Girls; dreams about stupendous
Meals in Parisian restaurants:
Mystical dreams that can be
Interpreted in interesting ways.
I have only one dream that is
Always the same. I'm lost in
A huge foreign city where I've
Never been. I'm afraid I'm
Going to miss an important
Appointment if I can't find
My way. Someone very important
But I can't remember his name.
There are people in the streets
But they don't speak English.
I get frightened. I begin to
Run from street to street. I
Run faster and faster till I
Wake up. Where is that city?

ATTRACTED BY THE LIGHT

(for Vanessa)

This warm evening, a very small bug
Has flown through the open window,
Landed on my head and is exploring
My hair. It tickles, but like a Jain
I'll not try to kill it. One of God's
Creatures. And am I not lucky
That at 79 I still have enough hair
To seem attractive to the bug?
You to whom I'm sending these lines,
Do you still think of me, far away
There in London as you are?
For me you are still the light.

JAIN: *member of an Indian sect, a branch of Hinduism,*
which arose in the 6th century. Jains believe that
no living thing should be killed, not even a worm
or bug.

What is consciousness that it
Leaves us when most we need it
To save what little we have
Managed to construct? Will the
Pale torch of loving soon be
Sputtering out for me? The
Children joke at table whether
Grandfather should be buried
Or burned. What difference
Could it make? Does their humor
Mask any affection that will
Last when life takes them by
Their little necks and shakes
Them as it can, rich or poor?
Tell me a happy fable that
Off in a distant galaxy some
Creature with three eyes is
Watching over me? That can't
Be so, believe me, it's not so;
Walk up or down, turn right
Or left, it isn't so. We came,
We breathed a bit of air, we go.

DE CONTEMPTU MORTIS: *in contempt of death.*

A TROUBLING CASE
OF AGNOSIA

Some mornings, thank heavens
Not every day, when he gets up
And goes into the bathroom to shave
He's troubled to find that the face
In the mirror isn't his own.
Who is this stranger who has come
In the night? The intruder is
Definitely not himself, though
There may be points of resemblance,
His ears, say, or his color of hair.
Who is he? Has he ever seen anyone
Who looked like him before? not
That he can remember. Occasionally
There will be a reappearance
Of the uninvited visitor. He has
Begun to assign names to these
Repeaters: Long-nosed Jack,
Fat-faced Harold, who looks a bit
Like his own Uncle Harold, Willy
The Turnip. He's glad to see them
Come back, if someone has to be
There in the mirror. They reassure
Him that he's not entirely crazy.
But they are disconcerting.
Fortunately they don't follow
Him down to breakfast or out into

The street. They are only the
Mirror people. In a way he's
Getting rather fond of them,
Would miss them if they moved
To the house of someone else.

AGNOSIA: *in psychopathology, loss of the
ability to recognize familiar persons or
objects.*

IMPRISONED

(for Gertrude)

It has been a long sentence for you
In the prison of my gloom
Where I sit scribbling verses
In my untidy room.

I could read to you from old books,
But what would that avail?
You're of the merry world,
I of my lonely cell.

Do you ever suspect how much I love you,
For that is what is true,
As I scribble my quare rhymes,
Rhymes that I make for you.

QUARE: *Irish dialect, queer.*

A WINTER'S NIGHT

The outside, where the snow
Is softly and soundlessly
Falling (there is no wind
Tonight) has brought its quiet
Into the house that was noisy
All day with TV voices,
The telephone ringing,
And the happy shouts of children
Romping from room to room.
Now, except for me, sleep
Has taken over the house.
I bring the silence of the dark
Outside into it. I wrap that
Around my cares. Soon I too
Will be sleeping.

THE LONGEST YEAR

Began with snowstorms, one after another.
In March a frantic night of wind took down
The huge sugar maple that showed a hundred
Rings when it was cut up for firewood.
Spring was dubious and too short, a hot
Summer too long. A child drowned in Tobey
Pond, it was horrible. Only in October
Were there a few perfect days with the leaves
Ablaze. Again before its time, baleful winter
Set in. Cars skidded on the icy roads.
At Christmas a false thaw deceived us
For a week before a deadly ice storm had
The branches of the trees cracking like
Rifle shots as they broke off all night.
It was a battlefield in the woodlot
Next morning. I didn't count the days
Of that malevolent year, I only wished
Never to see such another . . . until,
Blessed miracle, it was true spring,
The lilacs blooming, the daffodils
Nodding, and you, Persephone, came up
From the world below to seek me out.

PERSEPHONE: *in Greek and Roman mythology, the
goddess of fertility. She was kidnapped by Pluto, god of
the underworld, but won the right to return to earth for
eight months each year. Her return symbolizes the
coming of spring. She is celebrated in the cult of the
Eleusinian mysteries.*

They all told him that happiness
Was just around the next corner
Or beyond the bend of the river.
It didn't matter that his face
Was a discolored, lopsided pumpkin;
His happiness was out there waiting
For him, his own proprietary bliss.
All he had to do was keep his nose
Clean as Jefferson specifies in the
Declaration. But as the boring
Years rolled by he came to realize
They had all been lying to him,
They were all liars. There was no
Kind of happiness, great or small,
With his name stamped on it. Such
A thing simply did not exist. It
Dawned on him that the name
Inscribed on his birth certificate
Was not the one his parents had
Told him; it was a man named Tartuffe.

TARTUFFE: *the pious hypocrite — scoundrel,*
swindler, liar, lecher — in Molière's play.

THE INVISIBLE PERSON

Life kept rolling her over
like a piece of driftwood

in the surf of an angry sea
she was intelligent and beau-

tiful and well-off she made
friends easily yet she wasn't

able to put the pieces to-
gether into any recognizable

shape she wasn't sure who
she wanted to be so she

ended up being no one in par-
ticular she made herself al-

most invisible she was the
person you loved so much who

really wasn't there at all.

AS LONG

as you don't fall in love with him
you won't be harmed
he'll be kind to you
he'll amuse you with jokes & stories

he'll feed you delicious dinners
he'll send fragrant blooms
he'll buy you baubles
but if you begin to have feelings
more tender than he deserves
run, run, run, for the nearest exit.

THE EXOGAMIST

Her thin right arm
the skin so white
and smooth (port-
manteau passions?)
soft startled eyes
glaukopis Kupris
eyes of the Kyprian
bread on the point
of a knife no exit
but enticing danger.

EXOGAMY: *marriage outside a specific tribe.*

CANSO

She's the wife of a man who lives
In the village, a decent enough sort
Of fellow. I see her rarely, we might
Meet in the street once a month.
But sometimes in the night I wake
From sleep and discover her near me.
I feel that her beauty is infusing me,
It's taking possession of me.
Without touching her I'm being joined
To her. (It's not a sexual fantasy;
There's no tumescence.) But there is
An enlacement. Not always but usually,
This bonding seems to be taking place
In the past. I see a small river
Winding through a green valley.
I see low hills. I see a towered castle
On one of the hills. In the cedared
Garden of that castle I see my lady
Seated on silken cushions. She is wearing
A peaked head-dress and a richly brocaded
Gown. Which *canso* should I sing to her,
One that tells of sad longing, or one
That tells of joy?

CANSO: *Provençal, a troubadour love song.*

SO ALBERTINE

wasn't a girl but a handsome
young taxi driver and after

his mum croaked he gave her
fine furniture to the male

bordello all that superb
writing came out of shall

we say a certain untidiness
but who am I to be censori-

ous *le raplapat se réplique*
diversement et le jin-jin se

jete comme nous le voulons.

ALBERTINE: *the girl Proust loved so much was really*
  a male taxi driver.
LE REPLAPAT . . . : *Paris argot; put modestly it says:*
  boredom copies itself in various ways and our
  heads lead us where we will.

HOMAGE TO FELLINI

Found Lines in 8 ½

Do you study what is printed
On chewing gum wrappers before
You throw them away? If you did
Perhaps you would have some
Knowledge to understand what
Life is about. Or if only every
Other word you write were the truth
Your time on the spinning ball
Would not have been totally wasted.
If I could answer your questions
I would, believe me, but since
I can't answer them, let there be
Dedication to silence. When will
The script be ready? When can we
Finally start shooting? Or is
There no film to be made?

FELLINI: *Federico Fellini (1920-1993), the great
Italian film director whose scripts ask so many
tantalizing questions.*

THE HITCHHIKER

Good Friday Spell

The innocent fool
Made wise by pity
Came through our
Village, but nobody,
Not even the children,
Recognized who he was.
He did no harm, he smiled
But spoke to no one
And no one spoke to him.
Perhaps he was with us
For only ten minutes,
But we were blessed.

*In Wagner's Good Friday opera about the Knights
of the Holy Grail, a main theme is the revelation
that the stranger, Parsifal, is the predicted "inno-
cent fool" who will heal the wounds of Amfortas,
the leader of the knights.*

THE LEAST
YOU COULD DO

he told her, would be to forget
your pride of ownership for an hour
and let her come to sit by my bed
for that fraction of time.
What could we say in an hour
that would hurt you, or would take
anything away from what you've had?
What looks could we exchange
that would harm you in any way?
It's more than ten years
since we were lovers; in ten years
we haven't seen each other.
Is it so strange that we want
to meet again for the last time,
to look at each other, to listen to
each other's voices, ever
so gently to touch hands?
It's the least you could do.

THE LOTOPHAGOI

Take care you may be drifting
toward a distant shore from

which there is no return no
not death but a land like

that of the *lotophagoi* (the
lotos-eaters) Odysseus found

them on the African coast
they were gentle happy peo-

ple who had tasted of the
fruit of the lotos which

made them forget who they
were and lose all desire

to return to their homes
or be themselves again.

*Nine days I drifted on the teeming sea/ before dangerous high winds. Upon the
tenth/ we came to the coastline of the Lotos Eaters,/ who live upon that flower. We
landed there/ to take on water. All ships' companies/ mustered alongside for the mid-
day meal./ Then I sent out two picked men and a runner/ to learn what race of men
that land sustained./ They fell in, soon enough, with Lotos Eaters, who showed no
will to do us harm, only/ offering the sweet Lotos to our friends—/ but those who ate
this honeyed plant, the Lotos,/ never cared to report, nor to return:/ they longed to
stay forever, browsing on/ that native bloom, forgetful of their homeland.*
                                        ODYSSEY, Book IX, 83–97
                                        Tr. Robert Fitzgerald

Adapted from the Tawney-Penzer translation of
Somadeva's *Katha Sarit Sagara* (Sanskrit, 3rd century A.D.)

Story of the Chandala Girl Who Wanted to Marry a Prince

In the city of Chidambaram there was a very pretty
Girl who was determined to marry a prince,
Even though she was a Chandala, the lowest of all the castes.
One day she saw the son of the king who was making a tour of
    inspection of the city.
She followed his entourage hoping her beauty would catch his eye.
At that moment a holy hermit came by.
The prince got down from his elephant and prostrated himself
    before the *sadhu*.
This showed the girl that a holy man was greater than a prince. She
    followed the *sadhu*.
Soon they reached a temple of Siva, where the holy man knelt and
    worshipped.
The girl made obeisance to the *lingam* and even dared to kiss it.
Then a mongrel dog ran into the temple, sniffed
Around and did as dogs do right on the *lingam*.
Was the dog superior to Siva? How could she wed a dog?
The dog ran into the street and she followed it
To the house of a young Chandala man she knew who was a carter.
The dog leapt up to greet the young man and licked his face.
That settled it, the girl was reconciled to her caste,
And her mother sent for the matchmaker.

There was an astrologer who would stop at nothing to
    make money.
He left his home province thinking he could do better
    elsewhere.
There he went about advertising his skill and learning.
He had with him his son who was nine years old.
He embraced his son in the town square and shed tears
    over him.
When the people questioned him the wicked man told
    them:
"I know all that is past, and the present,
And what will come in the future.
I can foresee that my child will die in seven days.
That is why I am weeping."
His words aroused the wonder and sympathy of the people.
On the seventh day the astrologer killed
The boy while he was still sleeping.
When the people saw that the prophecy had come true,
They believed in his mastery of the art of prediction.
They honored him with rich gifts.
He acquired much wealth and returned to
        his own province.

SADHU: *Sanskrit, ascetic or hermit.*
LINGAM: *Sanskrit, the phallic column in shrines under which Siva*
        (Shiva) the destroyer-creator god of Hinduism is usually worshipped.

HAIKU

Now when I open my electric
Shaver to clean it a fine
Gray sand falls in the bowl.

THE OLD MEN

From way back, from when
I first came to live here
In Norfolk, I remember seeing
The old men of the village
Trudging down through the
Main street to the post office,
Or the grocery, or the pharmacy,
To get their mail or do an
Errand for the wife. Old men
Who walked slowly, some of them
With canes, they were retired
And had no place to go in any
Hurry. They would gather by twos
And threes to chew the fat
Even if there was nothing
To talk about except the weather.

Now I have a cane myself and walk
Pretty slowly, especially
If the street is icy, as it was
This morning. Young Jack Thompkins,
Mel's boy, spotted me
On the ice with my cane and
Came over to ask if he could
Help me up the steps of the
Post office. I felt a bit
Foolish but accepted his offer.
He took my arm and we made it
In good shape.

IN THE NURSERY

I'm nearly 80 but my wife and
The servants look after me as
If I were a child of about 4.
I've forgotten how to read so
They read aloud to me, stories
About Babar the elephant and
Other animals that I like.
I eat what they put before me
But yesterday I spat out on
The table something I didn't
Like. Toys are borrowed for me
To play with from a neighbor's
Children. I like best a little
Yellow car that will run across
The floor if I wind it up. They
Took me to get my hair cut; the
Barber gave me a lollipop to
Keep me quiet from wiggling.
Today they gave me a pad and
Crayons to draw with. I've
Drawn all the animals I know;
A dog with five legs by mistake
Made them laugh. It's hard for
Me to remember. I know my name
Is Jack, they call me that, but
What's the rest of it? One
Day I heard them talking about

Me and the doctor who comes
To see me now and then. They
Said he said I should be
Myself again in a few more
Weeks, just keep him quiet
And be patient with him.

This morning at breakfast, when I meant to say,
"Where's the marmalade?" my voice said instead,
"Where's the drawbridge?" and later
At the post office, when I handed my package slip
To Betty, the clerk, I asked her please to
Bring my strawberries. "Where would you get
Strawberries in December," she asked as she
Brought me my package of books. You see about
Six weeks before I'd had what the neurologist
Called a TIA, a little stroke. "Nothing
To worry about," he said. "It's normal
At your age. Take an aspirin a day and
It will go away." But it hasn't. Some wires
Must be crossed in the computer in my brain.
At first when the words began to wander
I was frightened. Was I going crazy?
Then I was annoyed. It was an embarrassment
With strangers to have to try to explain.
But now I think the wanderers are funny.
I wait with anticipation to hear what
Curious malapropism will pop out next.
I jot them down on a card I keep in my
Shirt pocket to see if there is a pattern.
I'm going to rearrange them into a poem,

A poem that may turn out to be
A surrealist masterpiece as good as
André Breton's "Soluble Fish"
Or his "Communicating Vases."

ANDRÉ BRETON: *the leader of the French
Surrealist movement (1896–1966).*

BENIGNUS QUAM DOCTUS

The wise old neurologist at Mass General,
The one whom other specialists look up to
Because he knows all there is to know
About strokes, has taken away what strangely
I had come to consider a valuable asset,
That is my belief that I had had a stroke
Myself. And why did I imagine that such
An accident was an advantage? In the
Weeks after the supposed event I had
Learned to live with the fear of it.
I had come to believe that it settled
The problems of the debility of old age
And even the greater one of how death
Would come and the probable time
Of death's coming. The stroke became
A kind of assurance and comfort.

This kind and learned old man
Questioned me for nearly an hour
About my symptoms and medical history.
He had me walk up and down the corridor
To see how straight I walked, how much
My gait wavered. Then he gave me
The news that I hadn't had a stroke
After all. There were no indications
Of a cerebral accident. I thanked him.
"But Doctor," I asked, "if there was
No stroke why is my head so constantly
Dizzy, and why has memory deserted me?"

"I'm not a psychiatrist," he told me.
"But the condition you describe is
Often associated with a state of
Anxiety." I thanked him again and
Left the hospital, my head spinning
As usual.

Pride, covetousness, lust, anger,
Gluttony, envy and sloth. Anxiety
Is not in the list of sins. What
Have I done, or what was done to
Me in a comfortable life to be
Rewarded with anxiety? Could it
Be the unforgivable sins of the
Fathers, sins from which there
Is no escape?

BENIGNUS QUAM DOCTUS: *as kind as he
is learned.*

I was sitting here typing
At the kitchen table. Nothing
Special about that, it was just
Another sonnet. But suddenly
My neck began to wobble, at
First gently then more and
More violently. There was
No pain, just this strange
Motion. All at once the top
Of my spine gave way and
My head fell to the floor.
It bounced twice then rolled
Slowly down the hall toward
The living room. No pain.
No blood came out of my head
But it left a track of white
Powder, like flour or salt.
I was afraid to follow it to
Find out what it was going
To do next. I'm even more
Afraid to lift my hands
From the typewriter to find
Out what is now on top of
My spine where my head used
To be. What if there is
Nothing there at all?

THE DAY I WAS DEAD

The three hours I was
in the morgue when
they thought I was
dead but I wasn't
were the worst part
of my whole life
they had me tied
to a stretcher in
a box in the wall
and they couldn't
hear me hollering
I was getting so
cold I was near
to frozen dead
the way they found
out I was alive was
when they came to
do the autopsy
I think there's
been some mistake
one doctor said to
the other you're
damn right there's
been some mistake
I told them get me
some fucking brandy
before I turn into
a block of ice.

Seven Segments from the Long Poem-in-Progress

BYWAYS

A Note on the Metric

In composing the long autobiographical poem "Byways," a work-in-progress of which the pages that follow are segments, I am intentionally avoiding rhetoric and verbal decoration. I would like to achieve a tone of colloquial speech and a pace for fast reading. Let's call "Byways" narrative verse. It is certainly not lyric poetry. A friend has called it a suitable receptacle for recollections. I owe the metric to my old friend and mentor the poet Kenneth Rexroth. He perfected the essentially three-beat line in his travel poem *The Dragon & The Unicorn*, which I published at New Directions in 1941.

FROM BYWAYS

Prologue – the Norfolk Santa Claus – Dawn

Often now as an old man
Who sleeps only four hours a night,
I wake before dawn, dress and go down
To my study to start typing:
Poems, letters, more pages
In the book of recollections.
Anything to get words flowing,
To get them out of my head
Where they're pressing so hard
For release it's like a kind
Of pain. My study window
Faces east, out over the meadow,
And I see this morning
That the sheep have scattered
On the hillside, their white shapes
Making the pattern of the stars
In Canis Major, the constellation
Around Sirius, the Dog Star,
Whom my father used to point
Out to us, calling it
For some reason I forget
Little Dog Peppermint.

What is this line I'm writing?
I never could scan in school.
It's certainly not an Alcaic.
Nor a Sapphic. Perhaps it's
The short line Rexroth used
In *The Dragon & The Unicorn*,

Tossed to me from wherever
He is by the Cranky Old Bear
(but I loved him). It's really
Just a prose cadence, broken
As I breathe while putting
My thoughts into words;
Mostly they are stored-up
Memories — *dove sta memoria.*
Which one of the old Italians
Wrote that? Dante or Cavalcanti?
Five years ago I'd have had
The name on the tip of my tongue
But no longer. In India
They call a storeroom a *godown,*
But there's no inventory
For my godown. I can't keep
Track of what's in there.
All those people in books
From Krishna & the characters
In the *Greek Anthology*
Up to the latest nonsense
Of the Deconstructionists,
Floating around in my brain,
A sort of "continuous present"
As Gertrude Stein called it;
The world in my head
Confusing me about the messy
World I have to live in.
Better the drunken gods of Greece
Than a life ordained by computers.

My worktable faces east;
I watch for the coming
Of the dawnlight, raising

My eyes occasionally from
The typing to rest them.
There is always a little ritual,
A moment's supplication
To Apollo, god of the lyre;
Asking he keep an eye on me
That I commit no great stupidity.
Phoebus Apollo, called also
Smintheus the mousekiller
For the protection he gives
The grain of the farmers. My
Dawns don't come up like thunder
Though I have been to Mandalay
That year when I worked in Burma.
Those gentle, tender people
Puzzled by modern life;
The men, the warriors, were lazy,
It was the women who hustled,
Matriarchs running the businesses.
And the girls bound their chests
So their breasts wouldn't grow;
Who started that, and why?
My dawns come up circumspectly,
Quietly with no great fuss.
Night was and in ten minutes
Day is, unless of course
It's raining hard. Then comes
My first breakfast. I can't cook
So it's only tea, puffed wheat and
Pepperidge Farm biscuits.
Then a cigar. Dr Luchs
Warned me the cigars
Would kill me years ago
But I'm still here today.

Ne quid nimis wrote Terence
In the *Andria*, moderation
In all things. So I hold
It down to three a day:
One after breakfast, one
After lunch and one after
Dinner. A Bolivar is both
Stimulation and consolation.
They claim that what
Makes a Havana so mellow
Is the spit of the Cubans
Who lick as they roll them.
But the best leaf for wrappers
Is grown right here in the
Connecticut River Valley.

Yes, we have our wonders,
Our natural phenomena,
As witness the little man
In the Santa Claus suit
Right here in South Norfolk,
This when I first came
To live here back in 1930.
I forget his real name,
We just called him
The Santa Claus man.
Even in the heat of August
He'd put on his red outfit
And his white whiskers
And walk up to the green
From his shack in the woods
Where he lived on relief
To ask at the post office
For mail from the North Pole
But of course there never was any.

Everybody loved him,
Especially the children.
He'd get a bag of penny candies
(there were penny candies
in those days, they didn't cost
a nickel as they do now)
Handing them out to the kids
Who trooped after him singing
As if he were the Pied Piper
Of Hamelin and like Mr Finney's
Turnip that grew behind the barn
And it grew and it grew
And it never did no harm,
Mr Santa Claus did no harm.
He was our local hero.

People came from other towns
To see and talk to him.
He was written up all over
The state...then suddenly
He stopped coming to see us.
They found him dead
With his head bashed in.
The state police went through
Their usual useless motions
But found no clue who'd done it.
We buried him in the woods
Near his shack, which had
To be burned down, it was
So filthy, he had never disposed
Of his garbage all those years.

Whom the gods would destroy
They first make mad
And whom they most love

They rob of their reason,
Be it Oedipus who killed
His dad and slept with his mum
Or our beloved Santa Claus,
Now nearly forgotten.
Nobody believes me
When I tell his story;
But I have the news clips.
Does he sit up there now
On Olympus, another Ganymede,
Kidnapped like Ganymede
By the eagle of Zeus,
A cupbearer pouring out
The nectar for those
Drunken clots, the gods?
Who in the end will arise
From chaos to punish
And destroy them all?

And speaking of those
With whose destruction
The gods amused themselves
Notable was Dawn of Santo, Texas,
The most perfect face and body
That my eyes ever beheld,
Each part was sheer perfection,
Modeled on the Venus of Milo
And perhaps, who knows for no one
Ever saw her, the Kyprian herself,
She violet-eyed, born of the seafoam.
Dawn's father began tampering with her

THE KYPRIAN: *Aphrodite was born on Cyprus.*

When she was ten; she was placed
In a home where there were
Brutish boys and little education.
Escaping at fifteen she reached Tulsa,
Got a job in a topless bar,
Met men, too many men
Who could see only the body,
Not the person inside it.
At last came one who was decent,
A man from New York
Who treated her kindly,
Showed her respect, a good man.
He took her to New York,
Set her up in an apartment,
Sent her to highschool,
Got books for her to read,
Bolstered her confidence,
Taught her how to dress.

But the cruel gods, bent on her
Destruction, caused him to die.
Back to the start, to despair,
Again the slave of her body.
When I met Dawn she was
Damaged goods. She cursed me
As I talked kindly to her,
Saying I was like the rest.
But I persisted. If it wasn't
Love it was an obsession.
In the end I know I gave her
Some happiness, some release
From her bondage, when we were
In Italy and Spain together.
One night in Milan when we

Were walking back to the hotel
From a restaurant she began
To cry in the street, at first
Softly and then violently.
She told me I had changed her.
That night she was indeed
A changed person, tender and
Passionate. We were happy
In Rome and Barcelona.
But I had not reckoned
On the spite of the gods.
They were jealous that I'd claimed
One they thought was their own.
In Burgos, cruel Burgos,
She suddenly became hostile
And silent, then catatonic.
I put her in the hospital
But their drugs didn't help her.
She escaped from the hospital
And threw herself under a tram.

I buried her in the cemetery
Of the Campo Sagrado, a long
Way from Santo, Texas. When I
Went through her suitcase
I found she had been writing
Little poems. Strange poems
That made no sense but they had,
In some of the phrases,
A kind of surrealist beauty.

Ezra (Pound)

To Rapallo then I came,
That was in 1934, a student
Bored with the academic conventions
Of Harvard, wanting to get to the source,
To learn about poetry from the best
Poet alive, and you accepted me into
Your Ezuversity where there was no
Tuition, the best beanery since
Bologna (1088). Literachoor, you said,
Is news that stays news,
And quoting from some old bloke
Named Rodolphus Agricola,
Ut doceat, ut moveat, ut delectet,
Make it teach, move the heart,
And please. You taught me
And you moved me and you gave me
Great delight. Your conversation
Was the best show in town,
Whatever you'd ever heard or read
As fresh as when it first got into
Your head. The books you loaned me
Were full of caustic marginalia:
Fat-faced Frankie (meaning Petrarch)
Had an assistant to put the adjectives
In the lines, it didn't much matter
Where they were placed; and
Aristotle was Harry Stottle,
A logic-chopper but so good at his
Job he anchored human thought
For 2000 years; and Aristophanes was
Harry-Stop-Her-Knees, good stuff about
Wasps and frogs. You believed

You were a revenant of Sextus
Propertius, your favorite Latin
Poet, saying that Propertius had
Rip-van-Winkled from 16 B.C. and you
Rewrote the best parts of your idol
In English, bringing the old boy's
Ideas up to date according to
Your own predilections. In your
Study, to keep from losing them,
You hung your glasses, your pens
And your scissors from strings
Over your desk. You had two
Typewriters because one was
Always being repaired from the
Beating you gave them; your
Letters were often half full of
Capitals for emphasis. You read
My poems and crossed out half the
Words saying I didn't need them.
You advised me not to bother
Writing stories because Flaubert
And Stendhal and James Joyce
Had done all that could be done
With fiction. They say you were
Cranky, maybe so, but only with
People who deserved it, stupid
Professors busy killing poetry
And international bankers making
Usury and *i mercanti di canoni*
Selling arms to start another war.

You elucidated the Eleusinian
Mysteries which were a key part of
Your composite religion, all about

Dromena and the *epoptea* and how
It was the *epoptea* that sent sperm
Up into a man's brain to make him
Smart. You loved cats and the cats
Loved you. Some days we would
Walk up the stony *salite* on the
Mountainside behind town, through the
Olive groves and the little peasant
Farms where the cats were perched
On the stone walls; they were
Waiting for you, they knew you
Would bring them a packet of scraps
From the lunch table. You would
Call to the cats: *"Micci, micci,*
Vieni qua, c' é da mangiare"
(Here's something for you to eat).
One day when we were feeding the
Cats near the church of San
Pantaleone we discussed what you
Would do with your Nobel Prize
Money when you finally got it,
And you thought that a chef
Would be the best thing because
You were tired of eating at the
Albuggero Rapallo, but the Swedes
Never got around to giving it
To you, they were too dumb to
Understand the *Cantos*. And when
Henghes the sculptor (id est
Heinz Winterfeld Klusmann)
Walked all the way down from
Hamburg to Rapallo to see you
Because he heard you had known
Gaudier, and arrived half-starved,

You fed him and let him sleep in
The big dog kennel on the terrace
(since there were no extra beds in
The penthouse apartment) and
You took him to the yard of
The man who made gravestones
And got him credit for a block of
Marble, from which he carved
His sitting-down centaur, and you
Sold it for him to Signora Agnelli,
The Fiat lady in Torino; and that
Was the beginning of Henghes' fame
And good fortune (and the drawing for
The Centaur became the colophon for
New Directions). You said I was
Such a terrible poet, I'd better
Do something useful and become
A publisher, a profession which
You inferred required no talent
And only limited intelligence.

And after lunch you would
Stretch out on your bed with your
Cowboy hat shielding the light from
The window with the big Chinese
Dictionary on a pillow on your
Stomach, staring at the characters,
Searching for the glyph of meaning
In the calligraphy. And years
Later the professor asked your
Daughter to define your ideogramic
Method of composition in the *Cantos*,
And she thought for a moment and
Replied that you looked deep into

The characters to find the truth of
Them, which was a properly Confucian
Answer. So you wrote your own
Versions of the *Great Learning*
And the *Odes*, which horrified
The sinologists, but the language
Is immortal. And you loved to
Quote from Confucius that:
"Anyone can run to excesses, it is
Easy to shoot past the mark, it is
Hard to stand fast in the middle."

My Aunt

Most mornings at Robin Hill
When I was living there on the
Third floor, that was before
My first marriage and when the
Office of New Directions was in
Her converted stable, she would
Summon me to her second floor
Sitting room after breakfast and
Sit me down by the fireplace for the
Daily monologue which usually
Went on for at least an hour,
Without interruption for I wasn't
Expected to say anything, just to
Listen and absorb her wisdom about
Life, of which there was a large
Supply. This sounds very boring
But it wasn't; it was endlessly
Fascinating. How had nature or

Some divine agent packed into
This little woman (she was my
Father's sister) such an intensity
Of feeling and such a capaciousness
Of spirit. She would have been in
Her sixties then and there she sat
In her Chinese silk peignoir
At the little table by the window
That looked out over the gardens
(She had attended a horticultural
School; in those days young ladies
Were not sent to college). There,
She looked out at her beautiful gardens,
After she had finished her breakfast
Which consisted only of one uncooked
Egg which she downed in a gulp.
There I was, slumped in an easy
Chair (I was forbidden to smoke
In her presence) waiting for the
Lesson to begin, impatient to have
It over so I could get on with my
Writing but curious to know what
Would come from the lips of the
Oracle that day. And once she began
I was in thrall to her conviction.

These scholia took place long, long
Ago. My aunt has been dead for over
Thirty years. The great house and
Its gardens have passed out of the
Family. I am older than she was
When she was my teacher. Yet even
Now as I sit here typing, her figure
Is as clear as if she were still

Alive; she is standing in the doorway
Of my study, the not beautiful little
Woman with the insistent voice.
Her consuming love for me has
Penetrated time, it surrounds me
Like a sacred aura. She had great
Need of me, imperfect as I was.
She had no children of her own,
And I was named for the father
Whom she idolized. I was the
Receptacle. She was determined to put
As much of him into me as she could.

She had a store of stories to tell me
About her parents and the aunts and
Uncles, even about my great-grandfather,
Who looks so fierce in the daguerreotypes
In the family album; about his house
Where wide lawns sloped down to the
Allegheny River as it came through
Pittsburgh to join the Monongahela
To make the Ohio at the Point where
Once Fort Duquesne had stood. Trips
In the buggy with her father to the
New mills on the South Side, where the
Eliza Furnaces were named for one of
Her aunts, the flames rising out of
Them against the sky at night.

Character studies of beloved servants,
Irish if they were "inside," black if
They were "outside." When the riverfront
Property was sold to make way for
Joseph Horne's department store, a new

House, rather ugly, was built on
Lincoln Avenue in Allegheny, which
Was becoming a fashionable neighborhood
For the quality. And much she had to
Tell about her father's place near
Zellwood in the central lake country
Of Florida. It had begun as pine and
Palmetto land for shooting quail; then
He developed it into orange groves
And an elaborate estate. "Sydonie"
He called it, named for his wife
Sydney Page. There were avenues
Bordered with live oaks and flowering
Shrubs. There were trees brought from
Many parts of the world; greenhouses
And slat houses. A dairy herd of
Jersey cows. There was a power plant
And an aviary of exotic birds. Two
Small lakes and a boathouse. Twenty
Cabins (without plumbing) where the
Black workers lived. (Remember that
All this was built before there was
An income tax.) The house was in
Spanish style, white walls and
Red tile roofs copied from a villa
In Granada; terraces and courtyards,
Balconies & colonnades, bougainvilleas
Climbing the walls, separate apartments
For the families of each of the
Five children. There was, of course,
A track spur at the Zellwood station
For the parking of private cars.
(Today the place is a boarding school
For the children of missionaries.

Came the income tax and it couldn't
Be kept up.) The *Ariadne* was her
Father's two-masted schooner, crew
Of twelve, one of the prides of the
New York Yacht Club cruise. Each
Summer the cruise put in at
Nantucket harbor for a few days of
Onshore partying. That was where
My aunt met her consort, a Coffin
He was, a gentleman through and
Through, *sans peur et sans reproche.*
It was a long and happy marriage but
Without issue: the country gentleman
And the lady who loved gardens.

In her later years my aunt became
Interested in spiritualism. Through
A medium in Pleasantville she met
An angel in the beyond named Lester.
Lester was most sympathetic to the
Concerns of cultivated elderly
Ladies. It was a fervid correspondence.
My aunt would telephone her questions
To Pleasantville where they were
Communicated to Lester in séances,
His answers reached Robin Hill in
The medium's automatic writing. She
Consulted him about almost everything,
Except her investments which were in
The care of a banker in New York. The
Problems of all the young cousins
Whom she was educating, difficulties
With the servants, social problems,
Matters of conscience, her husband's

Health — it all went to Lester. It's
Clear from Lester's letters (I have
Them still) that he really cared,
Particularly for what they called
"Going on to greater understanding."
Reading over some of the letters
I find that Lester's advice was very
Good; he was a sensible angel. He
Was a great consolation to her. At
A certain point, when I was giving
Her a hard time, I became the subject
Of the exchange. She told him that
She was much worried about me. I was
Making girls fall in love with
Me with no intention of marrying
Them; what was to be done?
Lester's answer was very comforting
And rather accurate as I read it now
In the medium's jiggly script: "Don't
Worry, my dear, James will be all
Right; you have given him good
Values. It is normal for young men
To flirt, it's their nature. He will
Settle down soon and when the right
Girl comes along he will know it
And will make a good marriage. He
Will work hard and be a success in
His profession."

She went on to greater under-
Standing in her 86th year. The
End was hard for her but she bore
It stoically. There were more voices,
A clamor of Babel; a coming on of

Darkness, a struggle to hold the
Light; confusion and desperation;
Then bodily failures, waning of
Strength; days in silence, barely
Able to speak; the soul fighting
For life in her eyes; inanition.
Two of her men, young Leon and old
Theodore Sylvernale, the old man
Weeping, placing her gently on the
Wicker chaise longue; her black
Maids who grew up on the family
Place in Florida covering her
With blankets; she is carried, an
Egyptian mummy, out into the sun
In her garden to lie there for
An hour. She says nothing and
Seems to see nothing, moves not
Even her hand, is no longer a
Person.

The Wrong Bed — Moira

It was in London that I
Fell into the wrong bed.
I should have guessed she
Was paranoid but sometimes
You can't tell. She picked
Me up in the Gargoyle. It
Was the night Dylan tripped
And sprained his ankle so
Badly he couldn't walk. We
Got him to his place in a

Taxi, then went on to hers
In Chelsea. I think her
Name was Moira but I can't
Remember for sure now. She
Was a small girl, brown hair,
Lively eyes, nicely dressed,
An upper-class accent, quite
Chatty. She had some bottles
And we drank till we both
Passed out with our clothes
On. Next day, about noon,
She ordered a car with a
Driver and we drove down to
Bath. That's when the bad talk
About Americans started, but
I let it pass. She had friends
In Bath, a couple with an
Apartment in the Crescent.
We dumped on them; they said
We could have the sofa. We
Ate at a pub, then the drink
Began again. I think I was
The first to pass out. I woke
Up in the night. She was on
The sofa with the man. No sign
Of the wife, I went back
To sleep on the floor.

Next morning when the couple
Had gone off, they had a
Shop somewhere, she said,
"Well, you brought me down
Here, I guess I'd better
Let you have it." She sat

Down on the sofa and pulled
Up her skirt. By then I
Wasn't interested, but she
Jibed at me: "Come on, Yank,
Let's see what you're good
For." When that was over,
And it wasn't much, there
Was the only kind word I
Heard about Americans. She
Said, "You're better than
Most of the Johnnies around
Here." I should have left
Her in Bath to get herself
Home, but I felt sorry for
Her somehow. She was a mess
But sort of pitiful. I got
Her back to Chelsea. She
Didn't ask me in. The car
Hires ran me sixty pounds.

The Desert in Bloom

Why can't you remember the Nevada
Desert awash with bright-colored
Flowers when we camped not far
From Tonopah that April long ago?
It was soon after we had met in
San Francisco and fallen in love.
You were George's sister, the
Beautiful poet's beautiful sister,
That's how I got to know you.
Surely you must remember how the

Desert that was so harsh all the
Rest of the year, rocks and gray
Sand, had suddenly burst into
Bloom, a salute to Persephone in
Almost violent praise of spring,
A salute that would last only a
Few weeks till the snow moisture
In the ground would be exhausted.
Rexroth had loaned us a tent and
We gathered dry cactus to cook
Over an open fire. At night we
Heard the soft cooing of doves
From all around us in the dark
But at dawn they ceased their
Complaining. You said that they
Reminded you of the doves in
Provence when you were there
As a girl, the *roucoulement des
Colombes* that the troubadours
And their ladies had heard in
The castle gardens, recording
Their sound in their *cansos*.

The ground was hard under our
Sleeping bags, the desert gets
Chilly at night, so cold that
Sometimes we had to squeeze
Into one bag, skin to skin,
Enlaced together. At night in the
Desert the stars seem twice as
Bright as anywhere else; when
We lay on our backs we would
Look up into the vastness, trying
To locate the constellations

And remember the names that were
Given them by the Greeks in the
Myths how many thousands of years
Ago. Andromeda and the Dioscuri,
Cassiopeia, whom Perseus saved
From the sea-monster; Orion, the
Mighty hunter; the Pleiades, whose
Comings and goings tell the seasons;
Berenike, whose pretty lock of
Hair has lived in song; the lion,
The dragon, and the swan. Your
People were Jewish but your
Beauty was more of Attica than
Of Phoenicia, great brown eyes,
Dark hair and olive skin. The
Girls of Lesbos would have adored
You but you were not of their
Kind. Your body is described
In the *Song of Songs*; not a
Fraction of an inch would
Have changed in its proportions
If I were a sculptor. The desert
Was empty and I would ask you
To lie naked in the sun, now
And then changing your pose, a
Moving sculpture. You had the
Marks of Eros, a girl fit for
The Mysteries. Liquid as the
Fountain Arethusa. And you were
Funny and endearing and passionate.
Holding hands, we took walks on
The endless desert before the sun
Became too hot. I picked flowers
And made a multicolored garland

For your hair. The handmaiden
Of Aphrodite, *venerandam*. In the
Shade of the tent I read you the
Exquisite love sonnets of Louise
Labé, which aroused me to make
Love again, hot as it was, the
Sweat glistening on our bodies.

One day we drove into Tonopah,
Now the slumbering ruin of the
Old hell-&-damnation mining
Town, where once fortunes of
Gold were won and lost at the
Tables, and men killed for it.
The streets were empty, but in
What is left of the Grand Hotel
California we found an old man
Dozing on top of the green
Gaming table; we woke him up
And shot craps with silver dollars
For chips. We stayed on the desert
For three days, when we had used
Up the water we had brought in
Cans.

Now after fifty years we're in
Touch again. You've had four
Husbands and I'm on my third
Marriage. You say that you
Can hardly remember our love-
Making on the flowering desert.
How can that be? For me it's
As fresh as if it only happened
Yesterday. I see you clear with

My garland in your hair. Now we
Are two old people nursing our
Aches. What harm can there be
In remembering? We cannot hurt
One another now.

Are We Too Old To Make Love?

Some fifty years ago, yes it was
That long, the summer when our
Families sent us to Munich to
Learn some German, and we met at
The opera in the Prinzregenten
Theater, you were wearing a blue
Dress and blue shoes with little
White bows on the toes, we had a
Few dates and liked each other
In a childish way. (I was seventeen
And you were sixteen.) We decided
It would be fun to put our bicycles
On the local train and go up to
Mittenwald in the foothills of
The alps. We rode around the
Mountain roads for several days.
It was lovely, such views of the
High peaks, except when it
Rained, but we didn't have much
Money so we would take one room,
But with two beds with those
Funny feather puffs on them
Instead of blankets. It was all
So innocent, like little children

Playing house. We never kissed
Or even held hands the whole
Time we were in the mountains.
You would undress and dress
In the inn bathroom and I would
Dress while you were out of the
Room. When we had spent all our
Money we went back to Munich.

We went to the opera a few
More times, we liked *Magic
Flute* the best; we took to
Calling each other Papagena
And Papageno and we whistled
The flute tune. We took walks
In the wooded parts of the
Englischer Garten. I suppose
I could have tried to kiss
You but I never did. What was
Wrong with me anyway? Soon it
Was time to go back to the
States to get ready for college.

You were going to Vassar and I
To Harvard. They aren't far
Apart but for some reason I
Never tried to see you though
I thought of you now and then
And we sent a few postcards
Back and forth. That was fifty
Years ago. You married a man
In California and had children
And now grandchildren. With me
It's about the same except that
I've been married three times

And had more children. Fifty
Years ago. Then one day there's
A phone call from a lady in a
Neighboring town whom I know.
She says that "your old friend
Papagena from Munich is visiting
And would like to see you and
Meet your wife. Please come to
Lunch next Wednesday." The thought
Of seeing you again excited me.
What would you be like in old
Age? My friend had said on
The phone that your husband
Had died a few years ago.
What would you think of me
With my head getting bald
And my old man's fat stomach?
I imagined all sort of things
About you, how you would be
And what we might talk about.
Some of these thoughts were
Not rational. I imagined you
Were still beautiful and that
I asked you, quite seriously,
"Are we too old to make love?"

Yes, I really imagined that
Question being asked and
Speculated on how you might
Reply to it. The meeting at
My friend's house was not
Embarrassing. It all went
Quite easily. You had white
Hair now, but you were slim
And moved gracefully. You

Still had your special smile,
A kind of enigmatic smile,
That I remembered. You and
My wife got along pleasantly.
We talked a bit about Munich
Days but not as if it were
Some big deal. Mostly we
Exchanged information about
Our children and grandchildren.

You asked about what books I
Was publishing. Up to that
Point it was all very
Easy, very comfortable. But
Then something happened that
Was astounding, something that
I still can't understand or
Interpret. We were alone in
The sitting room; the others
Had gone out into the garden.
You looked at me with your
Enigmatic smile and said, with
No more emphasis than if you
Were talking about the weather,
"You know, James, there's one
Thing I've always wanted to
Ask you if I ever saw you again;
Why when we were staying at
That little inn near Mittenwald
Did you tear the wings off all
Those moths and throw them on
My pillow?"

Is it possible I could have
done such a thing?

The Ancestors

And when we finally
Made it to Portaferry
Looking for ancestral graves,
Portaferry in County Down,
That is, an hour's drive south
Of Belfast, there was no trace
Left of the old hovel and
Potato patch, which they sold
In 1824 to take ship from Cobh
For Baltimore and the new life,
The two brothers, Alexander and
James, and the ailing old dad
Who was also James. No sign
Surviving as the parish church,
The fat little mayor told us,
Had burned with all the records
In '78. A pretty spot Portaferry
With a fine view out over
Strangford Lough, which the Danes
Called *Strangfjord* when they raided
There God knows when; and Joyce
Had told me my name meant Danish
Pirate and that we had last met on
The battlefield of Clontarf,
Cluain Tarbh on Good Friday 1014.

Disappeared without trace as if
They had never existed. The farms
And fields bulldozed, along with
The stone walls and hedgerows,
To make way for condominia
For vacation homes for Germans.

Fat Germans hiking around in
Lederhosen and Tyrolean hats.
So with the money from selling the
Place the brothers bought crockery
And a horse and wagon in Baltimore.
Heading west they sold the stuff
To the farmers in Pennsylvania.
There was enough to start a store
In Pittsburgh. It prospered and then
There was a bank. Then an iron foundry.
God-fearing people, Presbyterians,
Shrewd at deals, saving their money
To make more with it. Their luck was
The Civil War, selling rails
For the Northern armies as they moved
South. In the next generation
They sold pipe for the oil fields
In Texas, structural steel for
Skyscrapers, sheet for Detroit.

Five sons from James alone, five from
His son James, all working in the
Business. A Henry could draw and
Wanted to become an artist.
The old man would have none of such
Nonsense. No money in it. They built
Big houses on the hills of
Pittsburgh. God-fearing people who
Married their own kind, reproducing
Their own kind, until there was
Too much money. It spoiled most of them.
They moved east for the fancy living
In places like Long Island. They married
Rich girls from a better class.

Henry, my father, quit working
In the business at 40; he had been in
Charge of the company coal mines.
He devoted himself to golf, fishing
For trout and salmon, shooting birds
With an English shotgun; had his suits and
Shoes made in London, drove an
Hispano-Suiza; went to the races
At Auteuil and Chantilly, wearing a gray
Tailcoat and topper, as was the fashion;
Played *chemin de fer* in the casino
At Deauville, was often lucky at it.
Gave me a 30-foot power yacht
When I was 15, we sailed it up and down
The Florida inland waterway.
I called him "Skipper," he called me
"Mate." I loved him intensely. He gave me
The funds to start New Directions, though
He didn't understand the books I published.
His cousin, another Henry, got back to
Ireland by buying Castle Hyde. He rode
To hounds and kept fine horses,
One of which nearly killed him
By refusing a stone wall.
This Henry, the Boston one,
Once asked me, this was at lunch
At the Somerset Club when I was still
At Harvard, whether I was going to build
My life around skiing. "No sir,"
I told him, "I'm planning to be a writer."
"Not much money in that, I wish you luck."
Cousin Henry was right: no money in it
But a lot of satisfaction.

Tom Merton

When I first went down
To Kentucky to meet Merton
At Gethsemani, his monastery
Near Bardstown, the abbot
Had invited me for a visit
After I'd published *Thirty Poems*,
I was expecting gloom and obsession,
Grouchy old monks ponderous
In penitence, glaring through
Their sanctity...how wrong I was!
To be sure, the background
Was not prepossessing: a drab
Countryside, scrubby trees,
Dry fields, not verdant,
Shacks and billboards along the
Highway; the buildings
Of the compound behind
Its walls monstrously ugly,
Gray stone blocks set square
Without any architectural
Distinction, the spire
Of the church a tin spike
Poking up at the sky,
Over the gateway, in forbidding
Black letters PAX INTRANTIBUS,
It could have been a prison...
How wrong I had been about the inhabitants!
These brothers and monks
Were warriors of joy.
Happy and friendly, laughing

And joking, rejoicing in the
Hard life of work and prayer,
Seven services a day from Vigils
In the dark at 3:15 A.M. through
Lauds, Terce, Sext, None,
Vespers and Compline in the dusk,
These chantings of supplication
For the whole world, even infidels
Not just for the monks.
Such brightness, *lux in aeternitate,*

And Tom (his name now Brother Louis,
As a snake might shed his worldly skin)
The brightest among them, the merriest
Of them all, gaiety exuding
From him. One of the youngest
But already the intellectual
Pivot of the community with
His learning and his comprehension
Of what meditation is all about.
Tom never tried to convert me;
He said if I got grace
It would come from God
Not from his instruction.
He would answer my questions
About theology and the rituals
Very carefully, but no more.
One day we walked up
To the fire tower on the ridge.
Tom was the warden in fire season.
He was good at copping
The best jobs for himself.
He declined to join
The cheese-making crew

Or work in the fields.
And he got out of sleeping
In the dormitory by learning
To snore very loudly,
They gave him an abandoned
Bishop's room all to himself.
We sat in the shelter atop
The fire tower and chewed the fat
About the literary scene, what
The writers were doing. No papers
Or magazines came to the monastery,
The abbot only told the community
In chapter what was suitable
For them to hear. We arranged
How the books of the likes
Of Henry Miller and Djuna Barnes
Would be mailed to the order's
Psychiatrist, who would carry them
To Tom. On the morrow,
By dispensation of the abbot,
Who knew that publishers could
Produce book royalties to the
Benefit of the abbey, Tom
Had leave for the day to be off
With me in my rented car.

When we went out the gate
Past Brother Gatekeeper
Tom was formally dressed
In an old bishop's suit
With celluloid backwards collar.
But when he had finished reading
The day's lesson in his breviary,
And we came to a wood, he said,

Stop here. He hopped out,
Carrying a paper bag. I thought
He was going to pee, but no,
He returned in bluejeans
And an old sweater. Near Salem,
He said, I've heard there's
A good bar. We found it and
Inside, although it was only 10,
A goodly company of jolly farmers.
They looked askance at me
In my city slicker clothes,
But Tom, talking farmer and
Even randy, was an old pal
In fifteen minutes. I didn't drink
Since I was driving, but Tom
Was belting down his first beers
Since he became a novice:
One, two, three ... at four
I reminded him of our lunch date
In Lexington. Just one more, but
It was two more before I got him out.
Strangely, there was no sign
Of inebriation; he could have been
Drinking Coca-Colas. Our lunch hosts
In their little colonial
House-studio in Lexington
Were the Hammers, gentle
Victor, in his eighties,
In his youth a painter in
Vienna, doing elegant portraits
In the style of Cranach,
And later becoming in America
One of the great hand printers,
His *Hagia Sophia* of Merton's

Being perhaps his masterpiece;
And Carolyn, his wife, younger
Than he, a librarian at the
University who, under his tutelage
Had become also a renowned printer.

We ate in the garden, talking
About everything except modern art,
Which had to be avoided because
Of Victor's blood pressure.
There was a fine Pommard and after
Coffee Courvoisier, mostly consumed
By Tom but again no sign of his being
Tipsy. Our next stop, heading west,
Was Shakertown. No Shakers left
To do their ecstatic shaking,
But the old buildings and furniture
Well preserved. I started on the
Direct road home but Tom stopped me.
That ham, he said, I remember that
Wonderful ham laced with bourbon
I once had at the inn in Bardstown!
I turned the car and headed for
Bardstown. And it was indeed
A great Kentucky ham, a red-eye ham,
I think they called it, with a bottle of
St. Emilion to wash it down
And a few nips of cognac
To settle the stomach. And
Tom still sober as a judge.

When we got back to Gethsemani
There wasn't a light in the place.
Brother Gatekeeper was long gone

To his cot in the dormitory.
What to do? I remember, said Tom,
A place on the other side near
The cemetery where the wall
Isn't quite as high as it is here.
Tom was right, the wall was lower.
I got down on all fours
And had Tom stand on my back.
Can you reach the top? I asked.
Just with my fingertips, he said.
OK, hold on if you can,
I'll get up and push up your legs.
Tom was up, lying on the wall but
I couldn't reach his dangling hand.
I thought of my belt. I took it off
And tossed one end up to him.
Brace your legs around the wall
And I'll climb with my legs
The way Rexroth taught me on
Rock faces in the mountains.
Believe it or not, it worked.
We lay in the grass on the far side
Of the wall and laughed and laughed
And laughed. We have done the Devil's
Work today, Tom, I told him.
No, he said, we've been working for
The angels; they are friends of mine.
Keeping very quiet, Tom went off to
His bishop's room, I to my bed
In the wing for the retreatants.

INDEX OF TITLES AND FIRST LINES